8. 33

WATER

SCIENCE SECRETS

Jason Cooper

The Rourke Corporation, Inc.
Vero Beach, Florida 32964

Edited by Sandra A. Robinson

PHOTO CREDITS

All photos © Lynn M. Stone except page 4, courtesy of NASA

LIBRARY OF CONGRESS
Library of Congress Cataloging-in-Publication Data
Cooper, Jason, 1942-
  Water / by Jason Cooper.
    p. cm. — (Science secrets)
  Includes index.
  Summary: Provides a simple discussion of the different forms water takes, its importance to life on Earth, and some of its uses.
    ISBN 0-86593-168-2
    1. Water—Juvenile literature. [1. Water.]
I. Title. II. Series: Cooper, Jason, 1942-   Science secrets.
QC920.C66   1992
551.48—dc20   92-8810
                                                 CIP
                                                 AC

TABLE OF CONTENTS

WATER

Water is the most plentiful substance on earth. It covers most of the earth's surface.

Nothing else can change its form or move from place to place as water does. Sometimes water is in its wet, **liquid** form. Splash!

In cold weather, water freezes into solid form—cold, hard ice. Brrrrr!

Water also has an invisible form, called water vapor, when it is part of the air around us.

Most of planet earth is covered by water

WATER: SWEET AND SALTY

Most of the earth's water is in the oceans. Ocean water is **salt water.** It is so salty we cannot drink it.

The water we drink is fresh water, sometimes called "sweet" water. Most ponds, lakes and rivers are filled with fresh water.

The Arctic and Antarctic regions of the world have locked up most of the world's fresh water in great masses of ice.

A glacier in Alaska

WATER FOR LIFE

All living creatures—not just fish—need water for life. Water helps us grow and use the food we eat.

Water is important, too, for the way we live. Factories use water to make things that we use in our homes.

And water is important for **recreation,** or play time. Fish aren't the only ones who swim!

Water for recreation

WATER RISES

Water is used over and over again. Although we use water, we don't destroy it. All the water we use stays somewhere, but it does change form and place. And, sooner or later, someone uses the water again.

Water moves, for example, when the sun's heat causes it to rise invisibly into the air.

Sun's heat changes water into water vapor

Fog hides a Maine village

Snowflakes float onto a wolf

WATER FALLS, TOO

Water, or moisture, in the air cools and changes into droplets. **Fog** is tiny water droplets in a low cloud. Larger droplets, falling from clouds, are rain. **Dew** drops form at night from cooling moisture in the air.

Water that falls as rain on New York may have been in the ocean 3,000 miles away. So water is not lost. It just moves around.

Rain splashes Florida oranges

FROZEN WATER

When the air is cold enough, water freezes. Cold, falling water may be in the form of snow or little pieces of ice.

At the ends of the earth, in the cold places known as the Arctic and Antarctic, much of the ground is covered by ice and **glaciers.**

Cold weather changes water to ice

FLOOD AND DROUGHT

Rain and snow bring moisture to the ground. But few places have the same amount of rain and snow each year. Some places, like deserts, rarely have rainfall.

If water from rain or snow doesn't fall for a long time, it is called a time of **drought.** Sometimes too much rain or snow falls and makes floods.

Drought in the Florida Everglades

HOW WATER SHAPES UP THE EARTH

Water helps shape the earth. As water rushes downhill, it rubs against soil and rocks. It cuts and carves and digs. It carries bits of rock and soil away and leaves them somewhere else, making new land.

The action of ocean waves changes shorelines. Glaciers move rocks and soil.

Badlands of South Dakota, shaped by rivers and rain

WATER POWER

Stand near a huge waterfall. The sound of rushing, falling water is deafening. Imagine the wild, untamed energy, or power, of this beast!

We have been able to take the force of falling water and tame it. By using water power to run certain machines, we can make a different kind of energy—electricity.

Glossary

dew (DOO) — droplets of water that form on cool nights and settle on the ground

drought (DROWT) — a time of little or no rainfall

fog (FAHG) — a low, moist cloud

glacier (GLAY shur) — a slow-moving river of ice

liquid (LIH kwid) — something that flows freely, like water

recreation (rek ree A shun) — time spent at play or the play itself

salt water (SAWLT WAW ter) — ocean water; water with a large amount of salt in it

INDEX